Pathways to Devotion IX
By Linda McBurney-Gunhouse

Published by:
Creative Focus Publishing
Winnipeg Beach, Manitoba
Canada

Cover artwork by Linda McBurney-Gunhouse
ISBN: 978-1-928071-12-9

Copyright © 2022 by Linda McBurney-Gunhouse
All Rights Reserved.
R6

Published by:
Creative Focus Publishing
Box 704
Winnipeg Beach, Manitoba
R0C 3G0 CANADA

Please visit our website:
www.creativefocus.ca

Contact us at:
info@creativefocus.ca

All Scripture is taken from the King James Version of the Bible, unless otherwise stated.

A Note from the Author

Pathways to Devotion IX is the ninth in a series of devotional books that continue to evolve. It has been just over ten years since I wrote the last devotional book. Many things have happened that have changed the world, not the least being the pandemic of early 2020. But one thing that has never changed is God and His many promises to all those who dare to believe in Him! In reading this book, I hope you find that it offers insightful inspirational reflections to encourage you as you journey along through life's many interesting and challenging pathways.

Many of the reflections are personal accounts of my discoveries about God, and how He fulfills my every need through thick and thin. At the end of each reflection, is a section called Application. Here, you are given a guideline for additional Scripture reading, prayer and further reflection. I invite you to use this book as a companion to your Bible, and treat is as either a daily devotional book, or use it as a guideline for small Bible study groups. I leave you with one of my favourite passages of scripture:

Psalm 23:1-3,6

The LORD is my shepherd; I shall not want. He maketh me to lie down in green pastures: he leadeth me beside the still waters. He restoreth my soul: he leadeth me in the paths of righteousness for his name's sake. Surely goodness and mercy shall follow me all the days of my life: and I will dwell in the house of the LORD forever.

Linda McBurney-Gunhouse
Winnipeg Beach, MB
Canada

Contents

Day 1 – No Need to Know Evil 1
Day 2 – Children of Light 3
Day 3 – Being Established 5
Day 4 – The Anchor of Faith 7
Day 5 – The Power of God 9
Day 6 – The Work of our Hands 11
Day 7 – True Freedom 13
Day 8 – A Repentance that Costs 15
Day 9 – Hang on to Your Liberty 17
Day 10 – Fruitful Land or Drought? 19
Day 11 – Beware of Idolatry 21
Day 12 – Loving the Truth 23
Day 13 – The Importance of Patience 25
Day 14 – Living by Fear or Faith? 27
Day 15 – God's Plans vs Man's Plans 29
Day 16 – Get The Word Out 31
Day 17 – The Line Up 33
Day 18 – Whom Will You Serve? 35
Day 19 – Overcoming the Dark 37
Day 20 – A Safe Place 39
Day 21 – Knowing the Future 41
Day 22 – A Test of Hearts 43
Day 23 – Where are Work Ethics? 45
Day 24 – The Gift of the Word 47
Day 25 – Higher Perspective 49
Day 26 – The Good, the Bad, and the Unexpected 51
Day 27 – The Need to Witness 53
Day 28 – Misinformation 55
Day 29 – False Humility 57
Day 30 – Best Laid Plans 59
An Invitation for Salvation 61
About the Author 62
Other Titles 64

This book is dedicated to my friends in the Interlake whom I've had the privilege to know and fellowship with through regular Bible Studies. Your faithful prayer support has helped prop me up through many a difficult time. This fellowship has been the greatest blessing that came as a result of the many prolonged Covid lockdowns.

Day 1 – <u>No Need to Know Evil</u>

But I would have you truly wise as to good, and simple toward evil. And the God of peace shall bruise Satan under your feet shortly. May the grace of our Lord Jesus Christ be with you. Amen.
Romans 16:19b-20 MKJV

During the pandemic, I was receiving many different videos, write-ups, blogs and so on about an insidious plan behind the pandemic. One of the key words was "globalists," people who can't wait to get Satan's agenda going so that the anti-Christ can step in and try to wipe out Christ and Christians from the face of the earth.

For all intensive purposes, given the way the medical heads and governments have handled vaccine mandates practically forcing it on the entire population or else, makes me pause and see something diabolical going on—stripping people of rights with lockdowns, making us afraid of each other, wearing masks, taking jobs away, and so on. And the way they stirred up mass hysteria and fear over this virus that has a 99% rate of recovery, I have wondered many times if there is more going on than meets the eye. The facts, once researched, are very different than what the news portrays. In fact, the way officials have handled the entire pandemic has created catastrophic social, spiritual, and economic disaster, etc. on a global level.

For me, reading the news, and reading some of the information about the globalists have left me depressed, sad, frustrated, and discouraged. Then I realize that I can't soak up this kind of information, and neglect the very life-giving, positive, and faith-filled Scriptures provided in the Word of God, the Bible. I don't need to know such devastating information, do I? In fact, I thought we as Christians, the Bride of Christ, were to look up for the

Day 1

return of our groom, Jesus Christ, and look forward to the rapture with eager anticipation.

God will tell us what we need to know. Some might think this is ignorance and naivety, but it isn't. It is simply bringing ALL glory to God and not looking for something satanic when clearly God is in control. I think the next two verses really capture it well:

> *For he that will love life, and see good days, let him refrain his tongue from evil, and his lips that they speak no guile: Let him eschew evil, and do good; let him seek peace, and ensue it. 1 Peter 3:10-11*

As well, the opening verses from Romans 16 really speak to me about where my thoughts need to be focused. I need to focus on what is good, not what is evil. I like to think that instead of focusing on the future, I need to focus on the here and now, on the moments in today. For God is not through with using us here just yet. We still have work to do, and so we need to focus on doing good. Most importantly, we need to listen up to see what the Holy Spirit is saying to us.

Application

Read: Philippians 4:6-9

Pray: Pray for the Lord's will to be done on earth; and pray for His peace if you feel disturbed or uneasy when you read the news.

Reflect: What do you feel God would have you know, if not the negative news of the world?

Day 2 – <u>Children of Light</u>

For ye were sometimes darkness, but now are ye light in the Lord: walk as children of light: Ephesians 5:8

Further to the topic of yesterday's devotional about knowing evil, the Lord has taken me a step further. He clearly spoke to me about using caution when associating with people who are sending me all kinds of messages about the globalists and doctors who are silenced, etc. It has become clearer to me that all this information is not helpful, and that He doesn't want me involved in it right now. How do I know this? Because it has invited a wrong spirit. I have been so oppressed by it all, that I have been losing sleep. This is anti-Godly, and I need to get back into the light and stay there. Our God is in control, and all these news pieces make me think evil is at the reigns. But I know that is an outright lie.

The original sin was the temptation to know good and evil, but it comes at a terrible price. I don't want to know Satan's strategy: that is God's department, not mine. He will tell me what I need to know (see 1 Corinthians 2:11).

Let's take a look again at the term "children of light." What does that mean exactly? If we look further, we see that the Lord expects us to walk differently:

For ye were sometimes darkness, but now are ye light in the Lord: walk as children of light: (For the fruit of the Spirit is in all goodness and righteousness and truth;) Proving what is acceptable unto the Lord. And have no fellowship with the unfruitful works of darkness, but rather reprove them. Ephesians 5:8-11

Verse 9 gives us the answer: goodness, righteousness and truth. These are the fruits of the Spirit. These are the fruits we should be looking for. And take a look at verse 11.

Day 2

Is reading about the devil's agenda communicating with the "unfruitful works of darkness?" Should be we soaking up such information, and for what purpose? Everything we need to know is written in God's Word. It also says to "reprove" the works of darkness. In other words, go into prayer and rebuke and bind the devil's work.

As children of light, we have a most important job to do. It is written here:

> *Ye are the light of the world. A city that is set on an hill cannot be hid. Neither do men light a candle, and put it under a bushel, but on a candlestick; and it giveth light unto all that are in the house. Let your light so shine before men, that they may see your good works, and glorify your Father which is in heaven. Matthew 5:14-16*

May we heed Jesus' admonition to us, and be faithful to let our light shine!

Application

<u>Read</u>: Ephesians 5:8-17

<u>Pray</u>: Pray for the state of the world and for God's will to be done. Pray for the fruits of the Spirit to reign, and not the devil's evil agenda.

<u>Reflect</u>: Write about how you feel as a child of light. Think about what that means, and how you should live that out.

Day 3 – <u>Being Established</u>

And of Zion it shall be said, This and that man was born in her: and the highest himself shall establish her. Psalm 87:5

    I was thinking a lot about travel ever since the world shut its borders because of the pandemic. Without making travel plans, my world shrunk and became local and regional. I had to re-think my location, and why I was living here in the first place. The Lord began to speak to me about being established, and why that is something very important! I recalled all the years we lived at our current location. The friendships we made, the ministry that ensued, the groups I joined, volunteer opportunities, businesses I ran. The list goes on and on of all the wonderful opportunities we've had here to try and make a difference in the lives of others. I am so grateful for that.

    This isn't to say I wouldn't have traveled if I could have. There were several years when we were unable to travel as we looked after ailing parents, and had to take care of a second residence in the city. Sometimes we just didn't have the time or the money to go any place far away. Sometimes work kept us from going away.

    I can't help but think that we would have missed out on so many benefits of being part of a community, the trips would just have been a short-lived experience that we'd soon forget! There are so many other benefits to being established if you really think about it. For one thing, when the Lord establishes you (you stay where He has called you to be), there is peace in your heart, there is growth in what you put your hand to do, and a contentment that can only come from your willingness to obey and stay where you've been called to be. But, it isn't always easy, especially if you are on social media and your friend sends a picture of a warm ocean scene, sunshine and they're wearing shorts and

Day 3

sandals; it's in the middle of January and you're at home battling cold weather, and there's a blinding snow blizzard keeping you stuck inside!

There are times when I think that travel is more like running away rather than staying to allow God to work mightily in His way and time. Sometimes I think that to travel is to run away from the trials of life. We tend to think it is better elsewhere, when in reality, it very seldom is, especially if we have not been led by God to be there. Some trips are just the opposite, they provide wonderful opportunities to meet people that become like new friends. We are to take advantage of every opportunity to do the Lord's work no matter where we are!

I still think about travel, but I'm not focusing on it like I once did. My goal is to live each day one day at a time, and look for the opportunities that come my way to make a difference. Reality isn't so bad when we let the Lord establish us. There is reward after reward when we're willing to bloom where we've been planted.

Application

<u>Read</u>: Proverbs 3:1-8

<u>Pray</u>: Ask God to establish you if you feel transient and without peace.

<u>Reflect</u>: Think about if you feel established where you are right now. What steps can you take to feel more established?

Day 4 – <u>The Anchor of Faith</u>

Thy mother is like a vine in thy blood, planted by the waters: she was fruitful and full of branches by reason of many waters. Ezekiel 19:10

As part of my daily reading, I go through a book of the Bible and read a chapter a day. Not too long ago I read through Ezekiel. A particular passage caught my eye and I got the idea for this day's devotional. It is taken from Ezekiel 19:10-14. What once was a strong tree fruitful by many waters was plucked up, and ends up being planted in a wilderness in a dry and thirsty ground. She has lost her glory and can no longer wield any influence.

My first thought had to do with the current pandemic situation. It goes without saying that this is a very difficult time for everyone. I don't think anyone is exempt. Life as we know it has not been fully restored. The pandemic doesn't seem to end. With the strong vaccine mandate and passports, it has literally split the country, if not much of the world. Not everyone is vaccinated, nor will they be. Families are separated. In many places, loved ones are not allowed to visit their loved ones or friends in the hospitals or nursing homes. Graduations, weddings, and even funerals have been delayed or cancelled due to the pandemic. Our social lives have taken a dive. Social isolation is at an all-time high, and so is depression, suicide, substance abuse and more.

The government and medical professionals are making decisions to try and protect people, but their decisions are often ill-thought. Too many situations have arisen that they couldn't predict; they have no control over outcomes. It is a shaky situation indeed; they promised freedom if you get the vaccine. Slowly, restrictions are returning and cases are increasing in spite of the promising vaccine that was supposed to be the ultimate answer and end the pandemic. This is leaving many

Day 4

people disillusioned and wondering when the pandemic will ever end.

It is at times like this, that we must stand strong in the midst of these storms that leave us so unsettled. This is not the time to shrink back and give in to fear. This passage in Ezekiel speaks about fruitfulness. Fruitfulness extends to many others, not just ourselves. Not only do we need to have faith for ourselves when times are tough, but enough faith to go around. We need to remain positive. And remember that God never changes. His Word is as true today as it has always been and will continue to be no matter what storms we may be going through.

What is the anchor of faith? It is taking God at His Word, and living by it, staking our life on it if need be. God never fails! Do we believe this? If you walk by faith, and apply its principles, you'll see the most incredible fruit evident in your life, and those around you will take notice, too.

Application

<u>Read</u>: Ezekiel 19:10-14

<u>Pray</u>: Pray for God to help you develop a strong faith that can benefit not only you but others as well.

<u>Reflect</u>: What are some times you were able to help someone in need because of your strong faith? What will you do today to help someone by using your faith?

Day 5 – <u>The Power of God</u>

And my speech and my preaching was not with enticing words of man's wisdom, but in demonstration of the Spirit and of power: That your faith should not stand in the wisdom of men, but in the power of God. 1 Corinthians 2:4-5

One of the most obvious errors of the way government officials have handled the pandemic is that they have made it their duty and obligation to decide what is best for the population. The problem is, are they making the right decisions? Take a look at 1 Corinthians 2 verse 5. Is there such a thing as "wisdom" of men nowadays? If they aren't following the Lord and His Word, they couldn't possibly manufacture an answer to end the pandemic, and yet, they keep claiming the efficiency of the vaccines are the answer. Unfortunately, we can see that clearly it is not the answer. Now booster shots must be administered, so three shots now, and maybe more later. And after two years, the pandemic rages on.

Paul warned against putting our trust in man's wisdom for good reason. Only God has the ultimate answers and He carries out His Word and His will with perfect speed, and He performs His work flawlessly. It is us who refuse to wait, and so we rush ahead and make foolish decisions in our haste to make life better for ourselves. We are always stopped short when we see that our ways don't work.

During the pandemic, God has spoken to me emphatically about putting my trust in Him. As mentioned in the previous day's devotional, faith is the anchor that keeps us standing strong in the midst of life's worse storms!

And what about power? Power means the capability to do something perfect and well, to provide solutions for EVERY SITUATION AND CIRCUMSTANCE IN LIFE no matter how difficult. To deny the power OF GOD is to slip into a

Day 5

fleshly weak stance, and rely on our own abilities and skills to get a job done. It means certain and utter failure. We cannot even obtain salvation on our own; we have to rely completely on the power of God to save us and keep us.

For the preaching of the cross is to them that perish foolishness; but unto us which are saved it is the power of God. 1 Corinthians 1:18

We need to make it the norm to live in the power of God. He has saved us, He keeps us, and He continues to manifest His power through us. When it comes to working, helping others, witnessing, fellowship, or whatever it is we are called to do on any particular day, let's ask for God's power to continuously fuel us. And let's believe for greater things, as we learn to live daily in the power of God.

Application

Read: 1 Corinthians 2:2-5;4:7,20

Pray: Ask God to reveal your heart to see where you are at when it comes to relying on the power of God. Then obey the Holy Spirit's promptings to change.

Reflect: Look up all the verses in the New Testament that use the word "power" and read up on them. Take notes when you learn something new.

Day 6 – <u>The Work of our Hands</u>

And let the beauty of the LORD our God be upon us: and establish thou the work of our hands upon us; yea, the work of our hands establish thou it. Psalm 90:17

The Lord has been speaking to me about the importance of being settled. Surely the world is on sinking sand right now. They are having little success with their plans to get rid of the pandemic. This is because they don't know what to do. They don't turn to God, so they are at a loss with this huge problem that only God can fix. And so the pandemic rages on, and we find ourselves in one lockdown after another. This creates untold anxiety.

There are many things that can shake our confidence and create a sense of constant un-ease, or anxiety, because things change too rapidly and we have no control over them. Sometimes sudden illness can create an ongoing sense of fear and anxiety. We are no longer sure of our abilities, and we are not sure when we will be well again. I believe, based on the above verse and many other verses in the Bible, that the Lord wants us not only to be established, but our works especially. This is in spite of living in a world that seems to be spinning out of control with unexpected changes.

What does this mean? To me it means to deliberately put down roots. You can only do this when you are sure of where you are, where you live, and you are sure of the work that is given for you to do, that you will be able to continue to do it without looking elsewhere. Such is the case where I currently live, work, attend church, and am involved in the community. I have lived here for many years and know and have met a lot of people. I am rooted here, and it's where I enjoy being.

More importantly, even though the world is on shaky ground, believers are standing on a firm foundation, and that is the Lord Jesus Himself. It is our faith in Him and the relationship (covenant) with Him that keeps us steady, secure, and filled with peace no matter what the circumstances.

Day 6

When I pondered the opening verse, Psalm 90:17, I prayed about its further meaning. I believe the Lord explained to me that whatever we do should bear fruit. It's not a static thing, do it once and you're done, nor does it fade away and diminish. It grows and multiplies and bears fruit. It is something that you enjoy, and will bring great pleasure and prosperity. It can be a livelihood, but not necessarily. It will be something that grows and causes you to grow, and it will affect others. God will bless you in it. Have you experienced this?

I know that He wants us to trust in Him and walk with Him, and be at peace in our lives. This is one of the wonderful benefits of walking with Christ. You always have a purpose no matter how small it seems sometimes. All it takes is a first step, and obedience, then watch the work you do prosper.

Application

<u>Read</u>: Psalm 1

<u>Pray</u>: Pray for the Lord to establish you and make clear His purpose for your life, especially if you are undergoing change.

<u>Reflect</u>: What is God's purpose for your life? Share your thoughts on what you think it is and what you'd like it to be.

Day 7 – <u>True Freedom</u>

The Spirit of the Lord GOD is upon me; because the LORD hath anointed me to preach good tidings unto the meek; he hath sent me to bind up the brokenhearted, to proclaim liberty to the captives, and the opening of the prison to them that are bound; Isaiah 61:1

Months ago, after people were double vaccinated, and received a passport which gained them entrance into sporting events, theatres, restaurants, and other recreational venues, in the course of conversation, people will mention that they got their life back pre-Covid. They talked about without this passport, you are restricted and not free to go to any of these places. These people had felt previously that their freedoms have been stripped away with so many strict government mandates, at least in our corner of the world. The passport changed all that.

I thought a lot about freedom in the past couple of months. Is it the government that controls our lives, and therefore our freedoms? Perhaps it certainly looks that way if they can deny you access to places simply because you didn't "obey" their authority and take your medicine like a good little boy or girl. If you don't, you will get punished! And in every way, this discriminating vaccine mandate has separated friends, family and all of society. I shudder to think of the aftermath once the pandemic is truly over.

For me, I have experienced various loss of freedoms my entire life, so this is not something that determines my happiness, my state of mind, or my future. My freedom is spiritually based and affects every area of my life. For Christians, we are supposed to be willing to lose everything and still love and serve our Lord and Savior Jesus Christ without complaint! Here's what the Apostle Paul said:

Day 7

But what things were gain to me, those I counted loss for Christ. Yea doubtless, and I count all things but loss for the excellency of the knowledge of Christ Jesus my Lord: for whom I have suffered the loss of all things, and do count them but dung, that I may win Christ, Philippians 3:7-8

Many Christians are persecuted and martyred in different parts of the world. We too are to not count our lives too important to lose for the sake of Christ.

The so-called freedoms offered by the world only offer temporary happiness, if that. True freedom is freedom from our sinful self, and it only comes from Jesus, as it says in His Word:

If the Son therefore shall make you free, ye shall be free indeed. John 8:36

We have a glorious freedom because Jesus grants it to us. He is the only One who holds the keys to life and death. When we turn to Him in repentance, He hands us the keys to life, and we are forever free from that moment on.

Application

Read: John 8:32-38

Pray: Pray for God to reveal any areas in your life where you need to experience freedom.

Reflect: Describe what true freedom means to you. How will you live out this freedom? Share your freedom with a friend.

Day 8 - **A Repentance that Costs**

And your tires shall be upon your heads, and your shoes upon your feet: ye shall not mourn nor weep; but ye shall pine away for your iniquities, and mourn one toward another. Ezekiel 24:23

One day in my daily reading of the Old Testament, I read Ezekiel 24:20-25. Verse 23, as quoted above, jumped out at me. It became clear to me that we are to mourn more for our sins than we do for any other personal losses, even loss of family, and in this case, our own children. When we fail the Lord, we need to mourn the loss of our obedience and our relationship to Him that has fallen by the wayside. This is more grievous to the Lord than anything else.

There is a phrase we read several times in the Old Testament: "Ye shall know that I am the Lord [your] GOD." Why is this repeated so often? Because God's children had no fear of God. They often chose the wicked ways of the world, and so He had to discipline them, and draw them back to Himself. It is difficult to experience true repentance from sin when we have a hardened heart. And paying lip service, simply saying, "I'm sorry," really isn't enough. We must abandon our sin completely and loathe it because it has separated us from the God we are to love with all our heart, soul and mind.

Through all the years I have read the Bible, it occurs to me that God's main concern is His own children and their relationship to Him; the ongoings of the world are secondary. The Old Testament talks about welcoming the needy stranger, and the heathen that the Israelites live amongst. Otherwise, all we read about the world we live in are warnings, and to abstain from the pagan ways of the world around us. In the New Testament, it talks about the world as something that is evil and is dark (read John 3:16-21). In John 3:16 it says that God loves the world so much that He sent His only Son to save the world. This is talking about the people, not the world system.

Day 8

I find it interesting, when you look at it, how opposite God's ways are to the world's ways. The world encourages us to be self-directed and self-reliant. Anything less is weakness, and seen as something negative. Contrary to this, God wants us to be dependent on Him and let Him guide every aspect of our lives. Most importantly, the quality and strength of our relationship with God lies in our absolute willingness to allow God complete access to the throne of our heart and lives. I believe this is what He will work on, and will continue to poke and prod there until we are strong in our resolve to love Him first and foremost above all else. I believe God allowed Covid, in part, as a means of discipline for believers to get their heart right with God. Oh boy, this feels so harsh, but as it says in 1 Peter 4:17, For the time is come that judgement must begin at the house of God:

May we be ever open to the loving discipline of the Lord and have a true godly sorrow for our sins. Anything less will invite discipline in our lives if we truly belong to the Lord our God.

Application

<u>Read</u>: Ezekiel 24:20-25

<u>Pray</u>: Ask God to reveal your heart, and be willing to repent of whatever He brings to light.

<u>Reflect</u>: What happened the first time you ever repented? Write about it and share it with a friend.

Day 9 – Hang on to Your Liberty

Stand fast therefore in the liberty wherewith Christ hath made us free, and be not entangled again with the yoke of bondage. Galatians 5:1

Entanglements with the problems of the world and the problems of others actually will drag us out of a peaceful place into a tumultuous one. It will rob us of our liberty in Christ. How does this happen? Well, we unwittingly enter a warring foray that is not ours to battle, and we lose the focus of our own God-given ministry and God-ordained destiny. If we have been watching the news and getting entangled in political battles with others, this is an example of becoming entangled in the affairs of this world. Rather than risk losing friendships, we need to pray for all those in authority, as instructed in I Timothy 2:1-2.

The following Scripture talks about a battle we are in, and the first part gives us a clue on how to conduct ourselves as "good soldiers." We are very simply and precisely to avoid the entanglement of getting too involved with worldly things.

No man that warreth entangleth himself with the affairs of this life; that he may please him who hath chosen him to be a soldier. 2 Timothy 2:4

What does entanglement mean? It means mess, predicament, tangle, muddle. It implies that it's hard to get out of it once you're involved in it. No question, we are all in warfare, but the Lord is speaking to me to walk away from dissension and other people's problems (ones that they haven't submitted to the Lord). This is very important since we can become so entangled with the problems of others that we miss the power of God and healing we need to remain in the battle. The problem with getting involved with the unsubmitted problems of others is that we fail to realize that other than pray for them, the solution is in God's hands and not ours. However, Satan may keep trying to pull us back into the problem, so we lose our freedom in Christ. We are trying to solve problems that were never ours to solve in the first place.

Day 9

Lay hands suddenly on no man, neither be partaker of other men's sins: keep thyself pure. 1 Timothy 5:22

In addition, we must be careful not to encourage others in their sin, even if that sin is unbelief. We cannot agree with them if it goes against Scripture. We must stay true to the Word of God and what He has and is revealing to us. If any relationship drives us away from God, then maybe it is time to part company. More importantly, we need to check our hearts and our lifestyles to see if we are in bondage to anything. Then, we need to pray about it. Perhaps we'll have to get rid of it altogether, depending on what or who it is. Our freedom has come at a great cost, the precious blood of our Lord and Savior. Let's ensure that we don't lose it because of our own lack of discernment, and because we are doing things in the flesh instead of the spirit. Let's ensure that we live life in the spirit and not in the old tired ways of the flesh.

Application

Read: Galatians 5

Pray: Ask God to reveal any area you are in bondage to.

Reflect: What do you need to do to gain your freedom? Write about it and make a plan of action you can follow through on.

Day 10 – <u>Fruitful Land or Drought?</u>

If my people, which are called by my name, shall humble themselves, and pray, and seek my face, and turn from their wicked ways; then will I hear from heaven, and will forgive their sin, and will heal their land. 2 Chronicles 7:14

At the beginning of the pandemic in 2020, the above verse came to mind many times. I kept thinking that it is up to the church to make the difference in the world, and this will eventually bring an end to the pandemic. After all, the world and all that is in it belongs to God. We own nothing, but everything is on loan to us as King Solomon discovered (see Ecclesiastes 5:15-16).

It just seemed to me then that many of us have been holding onto the things of the world so tightly that it has affected our spiritual walk with the Lord. I know I sure have had to re-examine my priorities since it all began two years ago. Sometimes it takes a catastrophe to see the error of our ways, or that we have strayed even slightly from the path where we started on. Little has changed, even for the church (true believing Christians, the Body of Christ), when it comes to putting other things ahead of God in our lives. Although the children of Israel strayed in unimaginable ways, serving other gods, and abandoning the God who had loved them and set them apart for His own purposes, we too can end up in the same perilous place.

I read the entire chapter of 2 Chronicles 7 to get a better idea of the context of verse 14. I believe that God is speaking here to the children of Israel who specifically have turned away from God, and their land had suffered because of it. How does land suffer? It ceases to yield fruit, it ceases to be a source of life, and it is eventually good for nothing since whatever natural calamities have struck, it will cease to produce. When Israel followed God's

Day 10

ways and especially loved and obeyed Him, prosperity was always the result. There are dozens of examples of this in the Bible. In fact, they were never promised a bad land of drought, dry dessert or disaster when they followed God's ways. Instead, they were awarded a PROMISED LAND, filled with milk and honey, and land that bore fruit aplenty, prosperous indeed.

Last summer in western Canada, we were plagued with drought. It rained only a few times and it was just a sprinkle. Fires consumed the interior of beautiful British Columbia, and then later came devastating mudslides killing several people. All this during a pandemic that has turned people's lives upside down, and many have died. Then we have also endured one of the longest winters I can remember. It is April and we have two feet of fresh snow on the ground. I have often referred to the opening verse in 2 Chronicles, I believe that the Lord will bless our countries and end the pandemic when Christians pray, repent, and in every situation, always, put the Lord first and foremost.

Application

<u>Read</u>:   2 Chronicles 7

<u>Pray</u>:   Ask God to reveal His Word to you as you read 2 Chronicles 7.

<u>Reflect</u>:   Think about and journal what 2 Chronicles 7:14 means to you personally. What will you do today to obey and follow the admonitions in that particular verse?

Day 11 – <u>Beware of Idolatry</u>

If ye then be risen with Christ, seek those things which are above, where Christ sitteth on the right hand of God. Set your affection on things above, not on things on the earth. Colossians 3:1-2

A topic I have often thought about is idolatry. The Bible talks about it as something that we need to crucify as part of the old life. Why is this so important? There are many reasons, but mainly it will steal away our affection in our hearts that should be reserved for God alone. After all, He is the only one worthy of all our love and affection. He died for us out of an undeserved favor and love, and He paid for us with His own blood. We belong to Him. We may not think about our relationship with Him in this way, but God considers us as belonging to Him since He paid for us with His own life. This is something we could never repay. Truly, we owe Him our life. Everything else pales to this close, loving, relationship that He wants with us, and is freely offering us.

For ye are bought with a price: therefore glorify God in your body, and in your spirit, which are God's. 1 Corinthians 6:20

I think about areas in my life where I have struggled for victory. One of them is travel, and another is wanting a big house. All in all, for me, what it comes down to is spending much more time in the Word and prayer, and less time thinking about or desiring other things. The battle starts in our mind and that's where Satan likes to mess with us, and he hopes we will act on the thoughts that he puts there. Also, through the media, we are bombarded with so much junk of the world we need to guard our minds – as simple as shutting off the TV, computer, iPad, or smartphone, etc. We need to renew our minds. I find that the more I read the

Word of God, the more truth gets into my soul and clarifies things for me, and cleanses me.

An old saying from D.L. Moody that rings so true: "The Bible will keep you from sin, or sin will keep you from the Bible."

We really have no excuses when it comes to what we love more than God. James makes this clear:

Let no man say when he is tempted, I am tempted of God: for God cannot be tempted with evil, neither tempteth he any man: But every man is tempted, when he is drawn away of his own lust, and enticed. Then when lust hath conceived, it bringeth forth sin: and sin, when it is finished, bringeth forth death. James 1:13-15

Admitting that we made something more important than the things of God is a start to our way out. No one but us chooses what occupies our thoughts, and then leads to actions. We do well to spend our time more wisely in the Word focusing on the things of God, and what matters to Him.

Application

<u>Read</u>: Colossians 3:1-10

<u>Pray</u>: Pray and ask God if there are any areas in your life that mean more to you than God means to you.

<u>Reflect</u>: Resolve to spend time in the Word, being sensitive to things in your heart that may be affecting your relationship with your God.

Day 12 – <u>Loving the Truth</u>

It is time for thee, LORD, to work: for they have made void thy law. Therefore I love thy commandments above gold; yea, above fine gold. Therefore I esteem all thy precepts concerning all things to be right; and I hate every false way.
Psalm 119:126-128

So many times, I've heard people say when it comes to witnessing, "You gotta' love them." That may be so, but in doing so, if you don't warn them of their ultimate fate without God (eternal death), are we actually sacrificing the truth for love? And what kind of love is it that fails to mention the truth? After all, it says:

My little children, let us not love in word, neither in tongue; but in deed and in truth. ***1 John 3:18***

Love is all-inclusive when it comes to the truth. God is truth and cannot lie; God is love and this is what He does. You can't separate His love and His holiness from His very character. He is pure and sinless perfection. He is the Truth itself.

Jesus saith unto him, I am the way, the truth, and the life: no man cometh unto the Father, but by me. ***John 14:6***

In order to know God, you have to know the truth. You can't just love a person by being nice to them, and not tell them the truth of who Jesus is. Sometimes it seems scary to warn people of what's to come if they don't repent. But this doesn't change the truth, does it? It is a fundamental truth that without God we will perish and be lost forever after we die.

Day 12

For God so loved the world, that he gave his only begotten Son, that whosoever believeth in him should not perish, but have everlasting life.
John 3:16

I remember as a small child, I had to memorize this and other verses in John so I would never forget. They had a great impact on me, too. That's what the truth of God's Word does. We may not want to hear it, but it has a tremendous impact and will save us when we pay attention to it and obey it. Years later, when I was 19, many verses I had memorized as a child became a reality to me because Jesus became real to me after revealing to me who He is. We need to give this same opportunity to others. We owe it to God and to others if we claim to love either.

Let's be honest. It is much easier to love people and treat with with the utmost kindness, and fail to deliver the gospel message to them. But a careful reading of Scripture will tell us we must do both. How about changing the phrase, "You gotta' love them" to "You gotta' tell them."

Application

<u>Read</u>: John 3:16-21

<u>Pray</u>: If you haven't done this yet, pray and ask Jesus to be your Lord and Saviour. If you have already done so, ask God to lead you to those who do not know Jesus yet.

<u>Reflect</u>: Write out your testimony to share with others. Tell them what the Lord saved you from and what He will save them from if they have not already accepted Him.

Day 13 – <u>The Importance of Patience</u>

Knowing this, that the trying of your faith worketh patience. But let patience have her perfect work, that ye may be perfect and entire, wanting nothing. James 1:3-4

If you're like me, patience is something I struggle with. Why do things seem to take so long to be fulfilled? Other than my education following high school, I seemed to have to wait for the perfect job, and at times just for a job! I waited for the perfect soulmate and the perfect living situation. Many things came together and they had the WOW factor, I know, because I waited! But it was never easy.

In my early career years, I was anxious as a writer to become successful as a journalist. Unfortunately, the stress of the high-pressure newsroom, and the fact that I had to write in such a way that twisted the truth ever so slightly (embellish it), I decided to free-lance instead. I was going to travel and write about my adventures, and I am still looking forward to doing much more of that!

I went through a time of working as an office temp. I also worked in sales. When I was between jobs, it gave me an opportunity to really spend time in God's word. Yet, at that time I was impatient and I was also striving to make things happen. The striving also made me anxious. This is when I would make mistakes that I later regretted, such as going out with someone I would never marry. I'd have to end the friendship eventually, and this would be heartbreaking. Sometimes my impatience had to do with finding jobs. I would hastily take a desk or factory job and not be able to physically handle sitting so long because I'd end up with severe neck pain from a previous car accident. Other times I just couldn't sit still. I'd get in the car and just drive but not really go anywhere. I'd come home and have to face the same problems I left behind. I spent a lot of time reading my Bible in those days, and I did learn to love the time spent with the Lord. I realize now

Day 13

I had to learn to wait on the Lord, and that paid off in many dividends later on.

The best example I have of patience (I should say patient endurance) was waiting for my husband to come along. I waited to marry and the Lord rewarded me with the most wonderful husband. We have enjoyed many years together, and our love for each just keeps growing. After this particularly hard experience of waiting, I think I now understand what James meant when he said about patience making you complete, wanting nothing. When you wait for God's answer, it is complete. He leaves nothing out. In fact, my husband was all that I hoped for, and so much more.

In the opening verse, notice the prelude to patience is the trying of our faith. It really boils down to learning to trust God throughout all the circumstances and events of our life. When we put our trust in God for the provision and the outcome for all that we hope for, great things result, and the natural byproduct is patience, something we all need to keep us focused on God's ways and not our own.

Application

<u>Read</u>: Romans 5:1-5

<u>Pray</u>: Pray for patience.

<u>Reflect</u>: In what areas are you patient? In what areas do you struggle to be patient? Write down your answers, then ask God to help you be patient where necessary.

Day 14 – <u>Living by Fear or Faith?</u>

And fear not them which kill the body, but are not able to kill the soul: but rather fear him which is able to destroy both soul and body in hell. Matthew 10:28

Ever since the Covid 19 virus was released in the world, reaching Canada in about March 2020, it seems to me that individuals all around the world eventually made a choice. That choice was that they would either live in terror, or fear of catching the Covid, or they would live by faith, unafraid, and amidst all the hysteria and crazy, destructive restrictions, wait it out, without panicking. Basically, in many cases, it appears that the fearful were the first in line to get the largely untested emergency vaccine believing in the efficacy of its ability to bring an end to the spread of the virus. Some believe our own immune system and herd immunity would do the same, and perhaps with far greater and better results.

In all honesty, the message I have received from the get-go and from the Lord Himself, is to not be afraid, and to live my life normally. I have been able to enjoy peace throughout this time, even as the headlines have screamed FEAR in nearly every story. How much of it was based on truth, or was it part of a propaganda agenda to see how easy it would be to frighten the masses and get them to comply? It isn't a far stretch to see that this is what happens in countries led by dictators. Fear is the best weapon to get people to comply. I still chose to respect the laws of the health authorities, even when, many times, I was tempted not to.

And yes, some people were and are understandably hesitant of getting the vaccine because it is largely untested. No one knows what the long-term side effects really are. Several people have died from it. And some vaccinated think they can more easily get the virus from the unvaccinated. Yet, it is proven many times over that you can still get the virus (and possibly) die from it even though you've been double vaccinated. You can also spread it around to others. I have main-line news stories with this information, and it is a well-known fact that everyone can get the virus and spread it.

Having written a book about faith (and fear) in 2020, my convictions run very deep when it comes to choosing to live a life of faith rather than fear and unbelief. To me, it shows respect and honor to God when we trust His Word rather than what the news media tells us (which I rarely trust). And trusting Him is the only way to have peace in our hearts. I choose my freedom from fear, and to trust God instead. God has been very faithful to protect me throughout all these years. And I believe He will continue to do so.

Application

Read: Matthew 10:22-31

Pray: Pray for peace in your heart and that God will reveal and remove any fear that may be lingering there.

Reflect: Think of the times you were afraid and prayed. What happened? What will you do today to rid your life of fear?

Day 15 - <u>God's Plans vs Man's Plans</u>

For I know the thoughts that I think toward you, saith the LORD, thoughts of peace, and not of evil, to give you an expected end. Jeremiah 29:11

Have you ever made plans and somehow, they never happened? Unforeseeable circumstances do that. They change our plans. In the beginning of 2020 (the last week of January), my husband and I took a wonderful two-week road trip to Arizona in the US. We had been planning it for months and we were very excited and nervous about it. We hadn't taken a big trip for about 12 years, so it was time! We saw the Grand Canyon and other ancient ruins in Arizona. I went to a town called Jerome and found some valuable family history. It was one of the best trips I ever experienced. We had fabulous weather once we drove out of Nebraska and headed south through Colorado and New Mexico. I am always so thankful that we were able to do this trip covering several states there, and back home again to Manitoba.

When we got home, I began planning for the next year's road trip. This time we would head either to the far southern tip of Texas, or go to Florida to visit my cousin there. But here we are two years later and this has not happened. Covid and our government has kept us locked up at home. We aren't sure what we can plan and when we can take a trip again without all the restrictions imposed on traveling.

I know that many others have experienced the same thing. All their plans have been turned upside down, cancelled, and for some, they find themselves at square one. They have lost everything — family, friends, job, and even perhaps, a place to live.

Covid may have changed many things, but it also worked for the good in God's great Kingdom. In Ottawa, a Truckers Freedom Convoy comprised of God-loving, people-loving, and

Canada-loving workers, went far beyond a peaceful protest to have our strict Covid mandates dropped. They reached out to people in need with a heart of love and many people gave their lives to Christ. Sadly, our government handled it very badly. Our PM ordered an Emergencies Act thinking it involved terrorism. Nothing could have been further from the truth. Of course some people naively believed what they heard on the news. They didn't hear the real truth from the truckers themselves. We must always trust the Lord and obey His plans, trusting Him every step of the way that He is working all things out for the good.

When it comes to plans, another thing I am sure of is this — when God is in it, the doors will all open wide. It won't matter what man does or says. It's what God does and says that matters. He knows the future and He'll reveal His plans when the time is right.

Application

Read: Jeremiah 29:11-13

Pray: Pray for God to reveal His will when it comes to your plans. Trust Him to answer your prayers.

Reflect: Was there a time your plans failed? What happened? What will you do when it comes to your future plans?

Day 16 – <u>Get The Word Out</u>

So shall my word be that goeth forth out of my mouth: it shall not return unto me void, but it shall accomplish that which I please, and it shall prosper in the thing whereto I sent it. Isaiah 55:11

In a world full of misinformation, I feel as if you can't trust what you hear anymore. A solid footing is based on good sound honest truth. Without that truth, many people, and whole nations are heading for disaster. And censorship has become popular, or wok, much to my great sense of alarm. You have to watch what you say and make sure you agree with the popular opinion, even if that group "think" is based on a powerful political agenda to herd the masses into submission in order to obtain greater wealth and greater power. We know who is behind it all. We are in a spiritual battle and Satan is feverishly playing dirty.

For we wrestle not against flesh and blood, but against principalities, against powers, against the rulers of the darkness of this world, against spiritual wickedness in high places. Ephesians 6:12

It is so comforting to know that we are not fighting people; we are fighting spiritual beings who are influencing and ruling ungodly people that are in authority. But, we have a tremendous advantage. Just look at what God gives His children! He gives us authority over the enemy and his demons!

Behold, I give unto you power to tread on serpents and scorpions, and over all the power of the enemy: and nothing shall by any means hurt you. Luke 10:19

If you are a committed born-again Christian, and believe the Bible, you are at a tremendous advantage. A great

Day 16

number of enemies will fall at your side (over 10,000) when you're on God's side (see Psalm 91:7).

When we take the Word seriously, fruitfulness happens.

If ye walk in my statutes, and keep my commandments, and do them; Then I will give you rain in due season, and the land shall yield her increase, and the trees of the field shall yield their fruit. Leviticus 26:3-4

Notice verse 3 above, "walk in my statutes, keep my commandments, and DO THEM." There is action involved. We must know the Word and obey the Word. Take note also in verse 4 that when God's people follow and obey Him, everything improves! There is peace, the land yields its increase, there is safety and security! And enemies flee!

The Word is active and accomplishes God's will throughout the earth. We must use His Word every chance we get, and speak our own opinion much less. The world is in a mess right now. Let's turn things around starting today.

Application

Read: Leviticus 26:3-8

Pray: Pray for God to cement His Word into your heart so you know the truth. Ask Him to bring people for you to share it with.

Reflect: Have you felt hesitant to share the truth in case it didn't fit in with popular opinion? Write about it. Make a plan to share, no matter what.

Day 17 – <u>The Line Up</u>

And I saw the dead, small and great, stand before God; and the books were opened: and another book was opened, which is the book of life: and the dead were judged out of those things which were written in the books, according to their works. **Revelation 20:12**

Last fall, I was outside raking the leaves and the Lord showed me something. He showed me all the people who are lining up to get the vaccine, so they can get into another line-up and watch their favorite hockey team, or their favorite football team. Some want to line up at the airport to get on a plane and fly to a favorite or a new destination.

There are many line-ups in this life, aren't there? I've lined up ever since grade school. I've lined up at fairgrounds, amusement parks like Disneyland and Disneyworld, later at grocery stores, department stores, banks, theatres, live performances, airports, football stadiums, and so on and so forth. It seems that I've always had to wait in line for something.

But the Lord also showed me what we need to be lining up for right now is to line up for the things of God. Line up to receive prayer, to receive communion, to give a tithe, or offering, or gift, to love and embrace someone who needs a hug! There are many people who need visitors, and who need to know someone cares. The Lord went even further, and He shifted my focus away from good deeds, and the things of this world, and instead, He showed me the significance of the greatest line up that will ever occur in the history of mankind. It is the line up to meet Jesus, where He is seated on the throne, and everyone will be judged according to their works. Believers will not be in this line up. We will line up for rewards instead, but our works will be tested by fire to see what sort it is. This may seem surreal or unreal, but

Day 17

it WILL HAPPEN. I have always felt a sense of fear and awe at the thought of standing before God and giving an account of my life and deeds. I hope I will live godly until that time.

I saw a throne and I didn't see Jesus's face. I saw people lining up and when they get to His feet, they fall down and worship Him, and proclaim Him as Lord. John saw something similar on the Isle of Patmos:

> *And I saw a great white throne, and him that sat on it, from whose face the earth and the heaven fled away; and there was found no place for them. Revelation 20:11*

The Lord spoke to my heart to remain faithful and true to Him. Keep doing the things He asks us to do. We need to be reminded to line up for the things of God, not for the things of this world. He is the only way, the only answer, and our ultimate destiny needs to be the One He alone is offering — a one-way ticket to be forever in His presence. One day, I want to hear Him say:

> *Well done, thou good and faithful servant ... enter thou into the joy of the Lord. Matthew 25:21*

Application

<u>Read</u>: Revelation 20:11-15

<u>Pray</u>: Pray for opportunities to line up to do good to those around you.

<u>Reflect</u>: Think about future line-ups for you. Write about the importance of the line-up to see the Lord.

Day 18 – <u>Whom Will You Serve?</u>

And if it seem evil unto you to serve the LORD, choose you this day whom ye will serve;
Joshua 24:15

We choose each day who or what we will serve. Did you know that if you have decided to be a follower of Jesus, that He will not share your allegiance with any other god? He will want your total dedication to Him, since He is totally dedicated to you. It's a very important close relationship that God wants to be reciprocal. The children of Israel, God's chosen people, frequently turned away from God to serve other gods, or idols. They mostly inter-married and took on the customs of their unredeemed spouse and families. They were so caught up in their pagan gods that they forgot all about the loving God who had redeemed them and called them by His name. It was a sad and tragic situation.

Similarly, we too may be easily enticed by the world around us, and also blend in with the unbelieving world we live in. We can also be influenced by their anti-godly agendas if we do not stay close to the Lord. This is what comes from the rebellious roots of mankind's original desire to live independent of God (thinking we don't need God), and it makes a steady progression down the wide path that leads to Destruction. It can be as subtle as being led astray by the news and misinformation so prevalent these days. What does this actually do? It takes our focus away from our God and puts it on the problems that are presented to us.

Perhaps we have all slipped and stumbled when it comes to choosing whom we will serve. What does it mean to serve the Lord? For me, it means a deliberate decision to take time to read the Word and pray every single day. My goal is also to create a quiet environment (which is not easy when you have small dogs needing attention and many other things to attend to), in order to listen to God as well. Another thing I like to do is play soothing and encouraging Christian music while I work. Sometimes I listen to a favorite pastor give life-giving Bible-based sermons. These help me

Day 18

to focus my thoughts on the Lord, and not on problems or worldly matters.

Choosing to serve God may cost us in the area of personal goals that are not directly related to our walk with God. It may mean less me-time and more God-time. This past winter I was unable to join a few groups that I had been regularly a part of for many years. Instead, I was involved in three Bible studies. My social life was certainly affected, but my spiritual life blossomed. I know I have yet to see the results of this time that has been wisely spent in the things of God. I am so grateful for the way things worked out even though I missed the people I had socialized with previously.

When we choose to serve God, He is able to open our eyes to the truth, and to deliver us from anything that has us bound. This includes what is behind the many current anti-Christ agendas. He will reveal the truth, and will bring us into victory again and again.

Application

Read: Joshua 24:14-18

Pray: Pray for God to help you choose His ways every single day, and the help to carry it out.

Reflect: Reflect on the above passages of Scripture, and write about your current decisions regarding your faith.

Day 19 - <u>Overcoming the Dark</u>

The light shines in the darkness, and the darkness has not overcome it. John 1:5 ESV

Lately, I have been hearing some very disturbing news regarding some ill-thought decisions our Liberal government is attempting to make. One of the things they are trying to push is their own agenda when it comes to abortion. They want everyone to agree with their political view and make it a law. Once they do this, our nation could certainly crumble under the tyranny of forcing such damaging political views on an entire nation. We know beyond a shadow of a doubt that this is against God's will. Decisions like this not only strip us of our God-given rights to choose what we believe, but in many ways, our world feels unsafe and spiritually darker than ever before. When you can't trust your leaders, the people who were voted in with the assumption they would do good with our money and resources, then your country is on a slippery slope to ruin as history records time and again. In a word, such a government plunges a country into darkness, especially spiritual.

But it just isn't my country of Canada, but indeed, all over the world. Needless to say, in these times of uncertainty and fear, we need to lift up our nations to God and pray for our leaders that they make sound decisions according to God's Word, which is always for our best good. And we need to consider that we can make a difference in this spiritually dark world. Jesus said to His followers:

Ye are the light of the world. A city that is set on an hill cannot be hid. Neither do men light a candle, and put it under a bushel, but on a candlestick; and it giveth light unto all that are in the house. Let your light so shine before men, that they may see your good works, and glorify your Father which is in heaven. Matthew 5:14-16

There are many ways we can let our light shine. It is to have a good attitude, to cheerfully lend a helping hand where

Day 19

needed, and to be kind to people and do what we can to brighten someone's day.

In my part of the world, it's physically dark in the long winters and the days are short and nights are long. I'm so thankful when Christmas approaches with all the bright lights around windows and trees that cheer us up and give us hope. But more than this, it is a celebration of Jesus birth and the only true hope and light to mankind that would ever be offered by a loving God. In the midst of darkness, Jesus brings a light, so bright that to this very day and for all eternity, it cannot be extinguished!

In him was life; and the life was the light of men.
John 1:4

What a glorious hope! Hold onto that light today and whenever you feel sad by the darkness all around. Know that it can never overcome us when we put our hope and trust in Jesus! Amen.

Application

Read: John 1:1-5

Pray: Pray about God's direction for your life when it comes to being a light.

Reflect: Write about a time in your life where God used you to be a light. What happened?

Day 20 – A Safe Place

He that dwelleth in the secret place of the most High shall abide under the shadow of the Almighty.
Psalm 91:1

When the Covid virus was first discovered, a great amount of fear accompanied it. A catch phrase used to this day is "stay safe." We were told by health authorities we needed to stay home, only go out for essential things, stop travel, wear masks, wash hands frequently to "flatten the curve." It began a way of negative thinking foreign to many people since it was laced with fear. Yet for others, they took it all to heart and followed the guidelines and rules to the letter.

Throughout the pandemic many felt safe wearing the masks, social distancing and so on. As long as we avoided close contact with anyone not of our own household, we should be able to avoid the dreaded Covid virus. Then when the vaccines came out, people mistakenly thought the vaccine worked as a shield to prevent them from getting the virus. Every indication proved that it was never able to stop the spread, only perhaps lessen symptoms. The vaccine failed to deliver, as now third, fourth and is there fifth boosters being offered? Ironically, the failed vaccine actually led to the demise of the many restrictions, although the federal government in Canada is dragging its heels on dropping theirs. And this demise has had many people worried. They are no longer led by the controlled guidance of the health officials and government officials, so they have lost their security blanket. They no longer know about the numbers, the spread, what to expect or what to do? To go out, to say home? Added to that is the unreal fear of catching Covid from someone who didn't get the vaccine even though anyone can spread it. Now the vaccine passport is pretty much redundant.

Day 20

For me, from the very beginning I had the assurance of God's presence and His Word. My paradigm of staying safe, at its roots, had little to do with what the health authorities said. I had already witnessed the safety that only comes from God many times throughout my lifetime, so I was prepared for this pandemic. Psalm 91 particularly stood out for me. Rather than see the worldly "safeguards" being offered (although I mostly did what they said), I saw the Lord Himself as the source of my safety. Here is a favorite verse that I often refer to:

> ***There shall no evil befall thee, neither shall any plague come nigh thy dwelling. Psalm 91:10***

This verse helped me through many moments when others were literally terrified and hiding from the Covid. There are many verses in the Bible that address fear. What is the source of fear? I believe it is demonic. But perfect love eradicates fear because God is so much greater than our fears. Where is your safety today? If you have been afraid, you can turn that fear over to God, and trust Him to protect you throughout the many storms in life.

Application

Read: John 4:5-24; Romans 8:15; 2 Timothy 1:7

Pray: Ask God to take away your fears and replace them with His comforting love.

Reflect: Where does your safety lie? Share any fears you may have, and give them all over to Jesus.

Day 21 – <u>Knowing the Future</u>

When they therefore were come together, they asked of him, saying, Lord, wilt thou at this time restore again the kingdom to Israel? And he said unto them, It is not for you to know the times or the seasons, which the Father hath put in his own power. Act 1:6-7

Ever since Covid seemed to take over the world and bring it to its knees, many shattering world events have unfolded as a result. Businesses have plummeted, the way we socialize has been narrowed and sparse, people aren't as friendly because they're worried and stressed out. And to top it off, Russia has declared war against her neighbour, the Ukraine. Gas prices have soared, and so have housing prices. People are concerned about food shortages because the Ukraine is a big supplier of grain.

To top it off, in my beloved country, Canada, there has been an eating away and deep noticeable erosion of our constitutional rights as outlined in the Canadian Charter of Rights, which was penned in the early 80s and became law. Our Prime Minister would not allow a peaceful non-violent protest of the continued restrictive vaccine mandates that have wreaked havoc in our society and cost people their jobs. In fact, our PM had the audacity to call it a "terrorist act." Anyone who knew what was really going on, knew that this was untrue. Many people noted that the mainline news left out what was essential to understand the situation. People that were actually there reported the true account. When he declared the Emergencies Act, many Canadians and the rest of the free world looked on in disbelief, knowing full well this was a bold and unnecessary move, never before declared by any other Prime Minister in Canada's history.

In light of the many disturbing events going on in our world today, many Christians are looking into Biblical prophecy and believe that everything is lining up for the seven-year tribulation, or the Day of the Lord, as mentioned in Scripture. They believe

Day 21

there are globalists who used the Covid as a way of controlling people with the use of draconian and severe restrictions. What comes next is the mandatory mark of the anti-Christ people must receive on their forearm or forehead. Maybe things are happening faster than we'd like, and it's both exciting and scary. Exciting because it means the Lord is coming for His people in the worldwide rapture; scary because you don't want to be around to witness the extreme discipline of God upon all those who have rejected Him (essentially giving them another chance to turn to Him). But is this where our focus needs to be?

In the opening verse, Jesus says no, our focus should not be on the things of this world, or the times, or the seasons. They are in the Father's hands. What should we be focused on then? I believe we are to reach the lost with the Good News of the Gospel. Jesus tells us to be ready as well. Ready for what? For His soon return! All the rest is in His capable hands.

Application

Read: Acts 1:6- 11

Pray: Pray for world leaders that they make good and right and godly decisions. Pray for Christians to focus on the job at hand of witnessing.

Reflect: Write about your feelings about the future. What will you do to be ready for the Lord's soon return?

Day 22 - <u>A Test of Hearts</u>

Let us draw near with a true heart in full assurance of faith, having our hearts sprinkled from an evil conscience, and our bodies washed with pure water. Hebrews 10:22

At the beginning of the pandemic, I prayed and asked God what was going on. I had the complete assurance that He was in control. It helped to have heard some prophecies a year prior so that it made more sense when everything started shutting down. God simply spoke to my heart and said, as the prophecies had stated, that He was testing people's hearts to see where our loyalties really lie.

One of the first things to shut down was travel, so that the virus wouldn't spread from country to country. Yet it did anyway. Another area was sports, and so there were no popular hockey games or football games. Stores shut down. At one point, in my province, even at the time of Christmas, you could only buy essential goods like groceries and hardware. You couldn't even buy clothes. You had to either shop online, or get a worker in the store to pick out what you wanted. It was so strange and inconvenient. And the worst of it was that with wearing masks, you couldn't smile or communicate very well with people. In some cases, you didn't even know who you were talking to if you didn't recognize their eyes or sound of their voice. It was a little like playing a facial recognition game of hide and seek.

If I didn't know that God was using this time period to check our hearts, and yes, purify them, and get our focus back on Him, I would have likely crumbled and fell. I know many did, and were profoundly affected by the lockdowns. Perhaps their god was the shopping mall, the sports arena, eating out, or the love of traveling. It is easy to let that happen when we neglect God and the things of God. I am so thankful for Zoom and our online Bible studies, online social

Day 22

meetings with family and friends, and for the most part, our church remained open when allowed.

During that time, it wasn't so much an absence of the things of the world, it was more a replacement of those things with the Word of God! In those two years, I found myself growing in the Word, nourished by its life-giving abilities, and having less of a taste for the things of the world that quickly pass away. It settled my heart as well. Unable to go very far, I learned to be content.

With the pandemic winding down, I don't know what state my heart is in, only God knows that. Hearts are resilient and they can change quickly and we are not even aware of it. We need to be very careful we don't neglect the things of God. It is a good idea to frequently ask God to do a heart check on us. Like the Psalmist David, we can pray the following:

Create in me a clean heart, O God; and renew a right spirit within me. Psalm 51:10

Application

Read: Psalm 51

Pray: Ask God to reveal your heart to see what changes need to be made. Do what He reveals to you.

Reflect: Write about your own response to the lockdowns and restrictions during the pandemic. Did it draw you closer to God, or further away? What will you do today to draw closer to God?

Day 23 – <u>Where are Work Ethics?</u>

Whatsoever thy hand findeth to do, do it with thy might; for there is no work, nor device, nor knowledge, nor wisdom, in the grave, whither thou goest. Ecclesiastes 9:10

Even though when Adam and Eve sinned and were expelled from paradise, there is something to be said for the new life awaiting them outside of the garden. Adam was given the task of continuing to tend to the agriculture, but he would work hard and it wouldn't come easy for him like it did before. Eve would be subject to her husband. Their sin brought untold challenges they wouldn't have had in the garden had they not sinned. And it began a new work ethic. If you want to survive in this world, you'll have to work hard. If you want to eat, you have to work. But is that such a bad thing?

I couldn't help but notice recently that there have been many jobs available, more than usual. I wonder if there aren't enough skilled workers, or if people simply don't want to work if they don't have to? I can't help but wonder if the government is partly to blame. They generously handed out CERB payments to anyone who was put out of work because of closures due to Covid. This went on for about a year I believe, or maybe a little more. When people get something for nothing, it can create a sense of dependence and a feeling of freedom from not having to go to the trouble of going to work each day. This can happen when people collect welfare or sick benefits for too long. They lose all interest in working.

And there are others who absolutely love working. I know a young employee in a nearby city who is working two jobs. His goal? To be able to afford to buy a house. He has goals and plans, and he's actively working to make sure he gets what he wants. I had to admire him because it's obvious he has what it takes to succeed in life. And life won't be easy for the younger

Day 23

generations. Fortitude, sticking with it, and having a good attitude will go a long way to ensure this young man succeeds.

Nothing ever came easy in my own life. I left home at a young age, and had to work to support myself. It wasn't easy paying for an apartment, groceries, a car, clothing and everything else. I did this too, while paying my way through night school to get my Bachelor of Arts degree. I had a good steady job as an office clerk, but it wasn't my choice career. I had to wait for a few years before God opened up a writing career for me.

I believe God wants us to work, even if the job doesn't seem very exciting or fulfilling. Working gives us a profound sense of accomplishment, that we belong to something, and we can look forward to getting that paycheque or even a raise if we work hard enough. Jobs provide us with goals in life. Goals are essential for us to have something to work towards.

But it is good to be zealously affected always in a good thing, and not only when I am present with you. Galatians 4:18

Application

Read: 2 Thessalonians 3:8-12

Pray: Thank God for your work. If you need a job, ask God to provide you with one.

Reflect: How do you feel about working? Why do you think it is important according to the Bible?

Day 24 – <u>The Gift of the Word</u>

So shall my word be that goeth forth out of my mouth: it shall not return unto me void, but it shall accomplish that which I please, and it shall prosper in the thing whereto I sent it. Isaiah 55:11

In the late fall of 2020, I was a member of a large women's Bible study in the city. We met on Zoom each week because of Covid restrictions. At the end of one of our sessions, the leader asked if there were any prayer requests. I told her to pray for me as to how to reach a fellow bowling colleague, Roger, who was in his 80s, and feeling depressed. I wanted to witness to him about the Lord. So, Karen prayed and she asked that I would know what to say and do and to perhaps give him a Bible. It stood out so strong for me to give him a Bible. I never would have thought of it. I got the NIV full Bible from my church (they have a stack to give out). I put it in a bag with two black face masks that I had promised Roger. And I put a little booklet in there called, "The Way to Heaven."

I went to the bowling alley the next week, and arrived about the same time as Roger. Roger kept saying he forgot his mask. So, I handed him the brown paper bag with handles and said, "Here Roger, I brought you the masks. And there's a Bible in there." He looked in the bag and his whole face lit up, and he said, "You brought me the masks? Thank you, I feel like hugging you!" I asked if he had a Bible and he said he didn't have one, and never had one! Then he added, "I may not be here next week because I'll be too busy reading the Bible."

I hope Roger did what he said because shortly after, the government shut down the bowling alley due to Covid. I never saw Roger again, because within a few short months, he died. I don't know how he died, but I have a feeling he knew he was dying. This news hit me so hard, and I was so grateful I had a chance to give him the Bible. I hope he read it and accepted Jesus into his heart before he died.

I must explain that I had known Roger for many years. He was a fellow journalist, and we had lots in common. I had seen him around town at many different events. He had a column in various community newspapers. He was very well known. I knew he took a very liberal viewpoint of all that is ungodly. We did not see eye to eye on many different issues. So, for Roger to have softened his heart at the end and willingly and gladly receive a Bible is a miracle.

I wonder how many people out there would gladly receive a Bible if they were offered one? I wonder how many are in their final days as well? Truly, everyone will die, but not everyone is ready. We can make a difference in a life by offering a free Bible. In a world where people are in darkness, they need to see the light of the truth of God's precious life-giving Word. This has been a lesson to me to come out of my own comfort zone, and take every opportunity to share God's Word, especially to hand over an entire Bible free of charge.

Application

<u>Read</u>: Ecclesiastes 55:8-11

<u>Pray</u>: Pray for God to show you opportunities to give away Bibles. Ask Him to open doors for you to give some away.

<u>Reflect</u>: Write about the first time you received a Bible. Prayerfully, make a plan to start giving away God's precious Word.

Day 25 – <u>Higher Perspective</u>

For as the heavens are higher than the earth, so are my ways higher than your ways, and my thoughts than your thoughts. Isaiah 55:9

About a year ago my husband bought a high-end drone. We are both fascinated to see buildings and landscape from such a high perspective, something you can never see the same from on the ground. His drone goes up as high as 5,000 meters. Where we live there is no end to enjoyable and memorable sites perfect for drone flying. There's a historic large in-land lake with characteristics of an ocean. We have an old water tower still situated in the provincial park. We have a marina, and a historic creek snaking through the north part of town just a few streets away from us. We are looking forward to summer so we can go to these places and fly our drones (I have a smaller one).

So far, we have captured an old house fallen down, and a quaint historic Anglican church in the country south of where we live. The cameras can be maneuvered to capture all sides of any structure. My husband took a video of the water tower, and beyond that you could see the large expanse of the frozen lake. You get an entirely different perspective of the water tower as you see it within the bigger picture.

The height from which we can see things reminds me of the perspective from which God sees things. He sees the whole picture, all angles of any given situation. He can see into the past, the present and of course, the future. We just see things from a very limited perspective unless we ask God to reveal the bigger picture to us. Have you ever had a situation where it seemed impossible to solve without divine intervention? That was how it was for me when it came time to get married and settle down.

I knew I was going to get married, but I didn't know any of the details. I asked God why it was taking so long. He spoke to my heart and said that it was because there were many details that weren't in place yet. And also, that many people would be affected in a good way by this union. There were other hints the Lord gave me, and this went on for about a year. I may have had to wait for it all to come to be, but when it did, it was like an out-of-control snowball spiraling down a mountain side, unstoppable. It culminated in a grand finale of dating for two days, getting engaged, and married a few short weeks later. It was a whirlwind romance backed by many years of a solid platonic friendship. I am happy to say that I married my best friend, and our friendship and love just continues to grow through the years.

I love that God doesn't think like us or do like us. His ways are infinitely higher, and He is wisdom itself. We never have to worry when we leave things in God's capable hands. He'll always have the right and prefect perspective and answer our many prayers according to our needs.

Application

<u>Read</u>: Ecclesiastes 55:8-11

<u>Pray</u>: Ask God for His perspective on a particular difficult situation in your life right now.

<u>Reflect</u>: Is there a time that God miraculously provided for you above and beyond what you imagined? Write about it.

Day 26 – <u>The Good, the Bad, and the Unexpected</u>

Giving thanks always for all things unto God and the Father in the name of our Lord Jesus Christ; Ephesians 5:20

Last fall (October 2021), I decided that it was time to get a small dog. I wanted a chihuahua mix, a very small dog I could carry with me. We checked online, and surprisingly, we found one almost right away. She's a Pomchi (part Pomeranian and part Chihuahua). I fell in love with her pointy ears and her gorgeous colouring of black, golden, and white. She's got the sleekest black coat with golden undertones. She has unique markings and little sandy color sun-beams above her eyes. I call her Arabica (as in the coffee bean). She learns very fast how to do things. She knows that when she's done something good, she gets a treat from the kitchen! She nearly trips me to get to it.

When Arabica turned four months, she was pretty much completely trained. She needed a playmate, so we decided to get her a puppy. We found a pudgy little Pomchi with the most gorgeous colouring, similar to hers, but his coat is patchy with black and golden spots, little half white paws front and back, and sweet innocent looking eyes. The most endearing pointy caramel-colored ears. He's a doll, and I called him Timmy (as in the coffee name Tim Hortons). They are a wonderful match for each other, and they play heartily! Most people, when they first hold Timmy, don't want to give him back to us because he's so cute and cuddly. This is the good part of owning dogs.

However, there's a downside too. They quite often get into all kinds of trouble. I'll see an expensive shoe being chewed on, or a piece of upholstery on a chair or couch being pulled apart. And I have to watch that I don't leave any tissues out, and never leave anything on the lower shelves, it will be an easy target for chewing whether its books, paperwork, shoes, or cords!! We

Day 26

discovered that Timmy is an acrobat. He can climb over his kennel and jump down! So, we usually just bring him when we go out.

There is also an unexpected part of dog ownership. You just never know what to expect from one day to the next. Some days are better than others. But each day there is always something to be thankful for. My Arabica, although destructive at times, really wants to be with me. She senses when I'm troubled, and she wants to comfort me. When someone else is holding her, she looks at me with a longing, and before too long, she is in the safety of mommy's arms again. Timmy is very emotional and knows when he's been bad. He is apologetic and wants to make it up to me.

In every situation, there is always the good, the bad, and the unexpected. And most importantly, there is always something to be thankful for. Sometimes the unexpected is the very best part of our day. Somehow it makes it easier to take the bad. We can apply a good attitude to every part of our lives: the good, the bad, and the unexpected.

Application

Read: Colossians 3:15-17

Pray: Ask God to help you see the good in every situation, and be thankful even for the bad.

Reflect: What situation in your life would you consider good, bad, and unexpected? Write about it.

Day 27 – <u>The Need to Witness</u>

But if our gospel be hid, it is hid to them that are lost: In whom the god of this world hath blinded the minds of them which believe not, lest the light of the glorious gospel of Christ, who is the image of God, should shine unto them. 2 Corinthians 4:3-4

I have been very blessed to have been raised in an environment where God is honoured and Jesus is talked about. That was the norm. More than that, I was encouraged to regularly attend church, Bible Study, Bible Camp, Daily Vacation Bible School (where I got saved at age 5), and finally Bible School. I also went to rally's, crusades, special music concerts and youth groups. At a very young age I was taught to witness, too. When I was maybe 11 or 12, a group of Bhai came to the community hall in our small town. They were trying to recruit followers, likely to line their pockets, and who knows what else. After their speech, one of the gurus, dressed in the traditional Hindu garb, cornered me, and tried to get me to sign up. I knew it was all wrong even then. I remember telling him that Jesus is the way, the truth, and the life. He didn't like that and he kept pushing me to join, saying "You've got to keep an open mind." I kept repeating, "Jesus is the Way, the Truth and the Life." I think he finally gave up.

Witnessing and sharing the Word was normal to me. Both my parents witnessed that way, and some of my mom's large family boldly and publicly confessed their faith every chance they got. Often, they would accompany their witness with a take-away tract. When in the train station in Vancouver, B.C., I saw my Uncle Albert only briefly before he turned to a complete stranger to help him and then joyfully tell him about Jesus and His love for him. I think the stranger was blown away, to say the least. Uncle Albert never pushed his beliefs. He just gently and ever so lovingly shared the love of Jesus with whoever would listen.

I am so glad God sent me to live where I am today, at a Beach resort. We live just down the street from one of the largest inland

Day 27

freshwater lakes in the world. Every year a crew build a long pier onto the water and this is where we congregate to meet our summer neighbours, and also guests who may be renting a cottage or camping in a nearby trailer park. I can't tell you the many times I have an opportunity to witness, as we drink in the panoramic sky and can't see an end to the lakeshore since it is many miles wide (12 from where we sit) and long (258 mi). Pelicans will glide over, and sometimes a canoe will lazily drift by. People are on vacation and they're relaxed and open to listening. Praise God for these perfect opportunities to share His love and salvation.

When it comes to witnessing, I always think about a person's final destiny, and whether or not they have given their life to Jesus. If not, the Bible warns many times over that without Jesus, they will go to a godless and fateful eternity. The very least we can do is offer them an alternative — the free gift of salvation through Jesus Christ our Lord!

Application

<u>Read</u>: 2 Corinthians 4:1-6

<u>Pray</u>: Pray for God to open doors for you to witness, then do so.

<u>Reflect</u>: What is your experience with witnessing? Make a plan to incorporate witnessing into your life as a vital step of obedience to God's command to us.

Day 28 – <u>Misinformation</u>

And be not conformed to this world: but be ye transformed by the renewing of your mind, that ye may prove what is that good, and acceptable, and perfect, will of God. Romans 12:2

    If I keep reading the news, all I seem to find is what is negative, confusing, and disheartening. Last fall the Canadian and provincial government locked down mainly the unvaccinated. At the time, it was more like a punishment under the guise of keeping everyone safe. The unvaccinated were treated poorly and without respect for their personal medical choices. They were barred from most public places: they couldn't eat in restaurants, attend theatres or sporting events, etc. In truth, the vaccine was never enough to keep people safe, and they believed that the unvaccinated were a threat to their safety. But the Omicron variant finally pointed to the failure of the vaccines, and that anyone could catch and spread Covid.

    At the time, I was terribly disturbed by it all, mainly because I could see how hurtful it was, and how it was dividing the country. Family and friends were now divided. Many people had lost their jobs with no financial back-up except their savings, if they had any. I had never seen such a dark cloud hanging over my beautiful "free" country of Canada. I asked the Lord about what is going on, and He said something that totally made sense, and filled my heart with the beginnings of hope. He said that it was a spiritual battle, a war against truth. It had nothing to do with the vaccine or Covid. It is an all-out war on truth, and fear is the catalyst to camouflage the truth. It's called Misinformation. Unfortunately, most people would believe the mainline news, a mere tool in the arsenal of Satan to spread misinformation. This is also true for alternative news sources, or conspiracy theorists. Are there any credible sources? I found a few that I believe are legitimate, but my ultimate source of truth is always God and His Word who cannot and will never lie.

    Fear is trying to take over, and anxiety and uncertainty. Fear is a spirit and it has fueled the whole Covid pandemic. Only a small

Day 28

minority have ever actually been affected by it, and died. At least this was true until the much milder strain, the Omicron showed up. Yet governments have shut down society. Fear has served to break up families and society. That has been the demonic purpose Satan has striven for. Someone we met in a nearby resort, Falcon, reminded us of what the Bible says, that perfect love casts out fear (I John 4:18). You can't fear when you're surrounded by love. So, the attack has also largely been against love – love for God and one another. Because of fear we avoid each other, which goes contrary to God's Word.

The Lord prompted me again to stop listening to and reading the false news. My job is to live by and share the truth of God's Word. Reading the news will mean I partake of the misinformation by taking it into my mind. Instead, reading the Word will transform me in this difficult time to be joyful and strong and pass that on to others.

Application

Read: James 1:21-27

Pray: Pray for God to reveal any misinformation that may be in your own heart.

Reflect: Have you felt misled by any news sources having to do with current events? If so, write about your experience, and what you plan to do to correct it.

Day 29 - <u>False Humility</u>

But speaking the truth in love, may grow up into him in all things, which is the head, even Christ:
Ephesians 4:15

One thing I have found these days is that people are being way too sensitive to the point that you can't say what you really think or believe. An example is Megan Markel and her sensitivity when she thought she heard someone in the palace say that they wondered if her baby would be black or white. Is there something wrong with this questioning? People take offence at the drop of a hat and you're not allowed to say anything.

This is something I felt that I should pray about, but before I prayed, I asked the Lord how to pray for the situation. I told Him it's so much harder to teach and preach the truth when people are so easily offended, and you have to watch what you say. The Lord showed me that it was a spirit, and it's called "false humility." Along with that spirit is fear and intimidation. This is to keep us from preaching the gospel because that's what we're commanded to do. We know that people need to hear the truth and that's the only way that they're ever going to be set free, and that they're ever going to be eternally saved and spared from the hell that awaits them.

I was able to pray strategically that these spirits in high places would be removed and bound, no longer able to spread these lies because Satan is behind all of it. I prayed for the media so that the truth will prevail there, and that truth will prevail all over the world.

As for false humility, this verse came to mind:

But those things which proceed out of the mouth come forth from the heart; and they defile the man.
Matthew 15:18

Day 29

It is true that what is happening is not based on truth of how a person really believes or thinks, because they're too afraid to say what they really believe or think. This is why the Lord called it false humility because that's not really who people are or really what they think. People want to fit in, and not be persecuted or singled out for disagreeing what their peers think and say.

We need to pray and search our hearts to see if there is false humility there. Are we putting polite courtesy above giving people the truth? To tell the truth is to love someone. To pretend to be someone we're not is to be a liar, isn't it? The Word says that if we hate our brother then we don't love God. We are liars and the truth is not is us. So this is a very serious thing. Let's ask the Lord to search our hearts and see if there be any wicked way in us that needs to be dealt with. Then we need to repent of any dishonesty. May God help us not to be fearful but to be strong and loving to people. I believe that they will respond with respect for us. May He help us to embrace honesty and to trust Him.

Application

<u>Read</u>: 2 Corinthians 4:2; 8:21; I John 4:20

<u>Pray</u>: Pray for God to reveal any false humility in your heart, or dishonesty, and be prepared to repent and make it right with God.

<u>Reflect</u>: Write about your experience with going against popular opinion. If you never have, explain why not. What will you do about stepping out and going against the grain?

Day 30 – <u>Best Laid Plans</u>

But he knoweth the way that I take: when he hath tried me, I shall come forth as gold. Job 23:10

Many times in life, our own plans get tossed aside and something else happens to take its place. Like today. It is April 13, and there's a blizzard going on outside. Yesterday, you could see the grass and the robins had returned. Now the ground is once again fully and completely covered in fluffy white snow. Trees are heavily laden and we are bracing for loss of power from the weight of the snow on the power lines.

It seems that the winter will drag on indefinitely now. I feel as if I can't move on with my usual spring projects — cleaning up the yard and spacious back deck, decorating the deck for my spa-like get-away, setting up the front yard for visitors and such, putting our three screen rooms up, and going through our collection of stuff to get it ready for a garage sale, give-away, or the garbage.

This year, and since last fall actually, has been nothing like I hoped it would be. First Covid and all the restrictions, then a long winter, and now a blizzard. I wonder if God is trying hard to get our utmost attention? When the weather is good, it is easy to get caught up in being busy because you can do so much more, and go to so many more places. There's an easy but busy rhythm to life. But when it storms, or even rains on our parade, it causes us to pause and turn our thoughts in a different direction. For me, it is writing, and often reading. Sometimes I tackle a craft project, or do some fine art paintings. Most importantly though, is the time set aside for the Lord, whether devotions, reading the Word and meditating on it, and/or praying.

We can get far too caught up in the things of this world and not even realize we have strayed away from the Lord. I found this to be true last fall and winter. I wasn't able to go out as much for one reason or another. I found myself spending more time in my personal devotions. Plus, I attended a ladies Bible study, and we hold a Bible study on Zoom. This became more than enough for me.

It reminded me of my Bible School days. There was no TV allowed. I remember that at the end of six months of being off the junk food fads of the world, how good I felt. I never missed any of those things of the world. In fact, when I came back into society, I was shocked at the degradation of the world, even back then. Imagine now how much things have gotten worse.

When we walk with the Lord, He shows us the way that He wants us to take. May we be ever open to any changes along the way knowing that all things happen for our ultimate good. Let's embrace these changes that come along unexpectedly as they surely will. And let's look for opportunities to grow spiritually instead of being frustrated that our best laid plans have failed.

Application

Read: Proverbs 3:5-6

Pray: Ask God to give you peace about unexpected events that have created unplanned changes in your life.

Reflect: Describe a time when your plans were changed beyond your control. What happened? What did you learn from it?

An Invitation for Salvation

Dear Friend,

I hope this book has encouraged you. Daily devotions only truly benefit us once we've given our heart and entire life over to the Lord Jesus Christ. If you would like to receive Jesus into your heart and life today, and also have the assurance that you will spend eternity in heaven with Him, please begin by saying this prayer:

Dear Heavenly Father,

I come to you in the name of Jesus. Your Word says, "Whosoever shall call upon the name of the Lord shall be saved" (Acts 2:21). I call on you now and ask Jesus to come into my heart, forgive me for all my sins, and cleanse me. I ask you to be Lord over my life according to Romans 10:9-10 — "That if thou shalt confess with thy mouth the Lord Jesus, and shalt believe in thine heart that God hath raised him from the dead, thou shalt be saved. For with the heart man believeth unto righteousness; and with the mouth confession is made unto salvation." I do this now — I confess that Jesus is Lord and I believe in my heart that God raised Him from the dead.

In Jesus Name,
Amen

You are now reborn! You are a Christian and a child of God! Be assured, you have taken the most important step of your life and God has reserved your place in heaven. He will always be with you and lead you into all truth (read Hebrews 13:5b; John 14:26). You will need to read the Bible on a daily basis to get to know Him and all the many promises He has for you. As well, don't delay in contacting a Bible-believing church where you will find fellowship with others who have also taken this important life-changing step. May God bless you as you continue on your new path of life and freedom in Christ!

About the Author

Linda McBurney-Gunhouse enjoys her life in Manitoba, Canada. She writes to help others and inspire them to overcome difficulties and achieve success in life. She also enjoys story-telling in the form of writing fiction. Linda has spent a life-time writing and honing her skills. She studied Journalism, English, and History and received both a BA and B.Ed. in English. She has a diploma in magazine writing. She has worked as a contributing editor for a community college and also as an editor for a community newspaper in Winnipeg. Her articles have appeared in national, city and community newspapers and one magazine. She has written and sold one radio play. She is an accomplished eBook author of several inspirational books, including five full-length fiction. Her readership is international, and some of her eBooks frequently reach the Top 100 in specific categories. Linda also writes thought-provoking blogs.

She loves to share her faith and how she has overcome the many challenges in life in a way that readers can relate to. She sometimes teaches Creative Writing, and she does special speaking. She sometimes does free-lance writing for the local newspapers. She has also facilitated her own writer's group in a local setting. She continues to expand her thought-provoking blogs and book-writing. When she is not writing, she loves to be involved in creating several mediums of art.

Other Titles by Linda McBurney-Gunhouse

Inspirational Books

When Love Is All There Is
Loneliness: The Pathway to Discovery
Victory Over Backsliding
Footpath to Freedom
The Journey of Oneness
Power Thoughts for Positive Thinking
The Power of Submission
Healing For The Wounded Soul
The Act of Decision-Making
Cures for Stress
Freedom Through Spiritual Discernment
Spiritual Leadership in a Fallen World
The Journey to Contentment
No Fear of Hell
Money: Master or Servant?
The Bible: Conformed or Transformed?
Healing & Hope for Child Loss
Essential Steps to Increase Your Faith
Making Sense of the Rapture

Biography

The Bonk Saga: A History of Memories
Called to Overcome

Other Titles

Devotionals

Pathways to Devotion I
Pathways to Devotion II
Pathways to Devotion III
Pathways to Devotion IV
Pathways to Devotion V
Pathways to Devotion VI
Pathways to Devotion VII
Pathways to Devotion VIII
Pathways to Devotion IX
Pathways to Devotion X
Pathways to Devotion XI

Fiction

The Redemption of Steep Rock Cove
Return to Steep Rock Cove
Christmas Comes to Steep Rock Cove
Waves of Change at Steep Rock Cove
Driving with the Top Down
Track Three

Poetry Books

Heart Songs
Songs in the Desert
Water Crossings
Wings I: Morning Arising
Wings II: Daylight Reflections
Wings III: Contemplation

Other Titles

Creative How-to Books

Artistic Ideas & Inspirations
How to Create Stories From Your Own Life
Living a Creative Life

Writing Manuals

Creative Writing
Write Your Life Story
Fiction Writing

Please visit our website at www.creativefocus.ca to discover the many books from this list that are available as eBooks.

Note: If you have enjoyed reading this book, or any other eBook of mine, please rate it online, or recommend it on your Facebook page. It will help spread the word, and let others know it is available. My goal is to help, encourage and inspire others through my writing. Thank you and may God richly bless you!

www.ingramcontent.com/pod-product-compliance
Lightning Source LLC
Chambersburg PA
CBHW061341040426
42444CB00011B/3037